STECK-VAUGHN
PORTRAIT OF AMERICA

North Dakota

Steck-Vaughn Company

Executive Editor	Diane Sharpe
Senior Editor	Martin S. Saiewitz
Design Manager	Pamela Heaney
Photo Editor	Margie Foster
Electronic Cover Graphics	Alan Klemp

Proof Positive/Farrowlyne Associates, Inc.
Program Editorial, Revision Development, Design, and Production

Consultant: Jeff Eslinger, Tourism Information Supervisor, North Dakota Department of Tourism

Published by Raintree Steck-Vaughn Publishers, an imprint of Steck-Vaughn Company.

A Turner Educational Services, Inc. book. Based on the Portrait of America television series by R. E. (Ted) Turner.

Cover Photo: Farmhouse and sunflowers by © Annie Griffiths/Westlight.

Library of Congress Cataloging-in-Publication Data

Thompson, Kathleen.
    North Dakota / Kathleen Thompson.
      p. cm. — (Portrait of America)
    "Based on the Portrait of America television series" — T.p. verso.
    "A Turner book."
    Includes index.
    ISBN 0-8114-7379-1 (library binding). — ISBN 0-8114-7460-7 (softcover)
    1. North Dakota—Juvenile literature. I. Title. II. Series:
Thompson, Kathleen. Portrait of America.
F636.3.T46 1996
978.4—dc20

                              95-50424
                              CIP
                              AC

Printed and Bound in the United States of America

2 3 4 5 6 7 8 9 10 WZ 03 02 01 00 99

Acknowledgments
The publishers wish to thank the following for permission to reproduce photographs:
P. 7 © Annie Griffiths/Westlight; p. 8 © Jack Hoehn Jr./Profiles West; pp. 10 (both), 11 State Historical Society of North Dakota; p. 12 (all) Three Affiliated Tribes Museum, New Town; pp. 13, 14, 15 State Historical Society of North Dakota; p. 17 University of North Dakota; p. 19 North Dakota Game and Fish Department; p. 20 State Historical Society of North Dakota; pp. 21, 22 Theodore Roosevelt National Park, National Park Service; p. 23 National Portrait Gallery, Smithsonian Institution; p. 24 © Julie Habel/Westlight; p. 26 (top) North Dakota Tourism, (bottom) © Jerry Bakke/North Dakota Wheat Commission; p. 27 © Dawn Charging/North Dakota Tourism; p. 28 National Pasta Association; p. 29 © Wiley Wales/Profiles West; p. 30 Jud Cafe Association; p. 31 Great Plains Assistance Foundation; p. 32 © Dawn Charging/North Dakota Tourism; p. 34 (top) State Historical Society of North Dakota, (bottom) North Dakota Game and Fish Department; p. 35 Knife River Indian Village National Historic Site, National Park Service; p. 36 © Ken Rogers/Westlight; p. 37 © Craig Bihrle/North Dakota Game and Fish Department; p. 38 University of North Dakota, College of Fine Arts; p. 39 (both) © Jackie McElroy; p. 40 Pioneer Trails Regional Museum; p. 41 (left) State Historical Society of North Dakota, (right) Pioneer Trails Regional Museum; p. 42 © Paul Gallagher/Profiles West; p. 44 © Dick Larson/University of North Dakota; p. 46 One Mile Up; p. 47 (left) One Mile Up, (center, right) North Dakota Tourism.

STECK-VAUGHN

PORTRAIT OF AMERICA

North Dakota

Kathleen Thompson

A Turner Book

RSVP

RAINTREE
STECK-VAUGHN
PUBLISHERS

The Steck-Vaughn Company

Austin, Texas

Pembina

Rugby

Williston

Minot

Devils Lake

GREAT PLAINS

Grand Forks

Sheyenne River

Little Missouri River

Lake Sakakawea

Mayville

THEODORE
ROOSEVELT
NATIONAL PARK

Missouri River

Carrington

Red River

Valley City

Dickinson

Mandan

★ BISMARCK

Jamestown

Fargo

Jud

▲ White Butte

BADLANDS

North Dakota

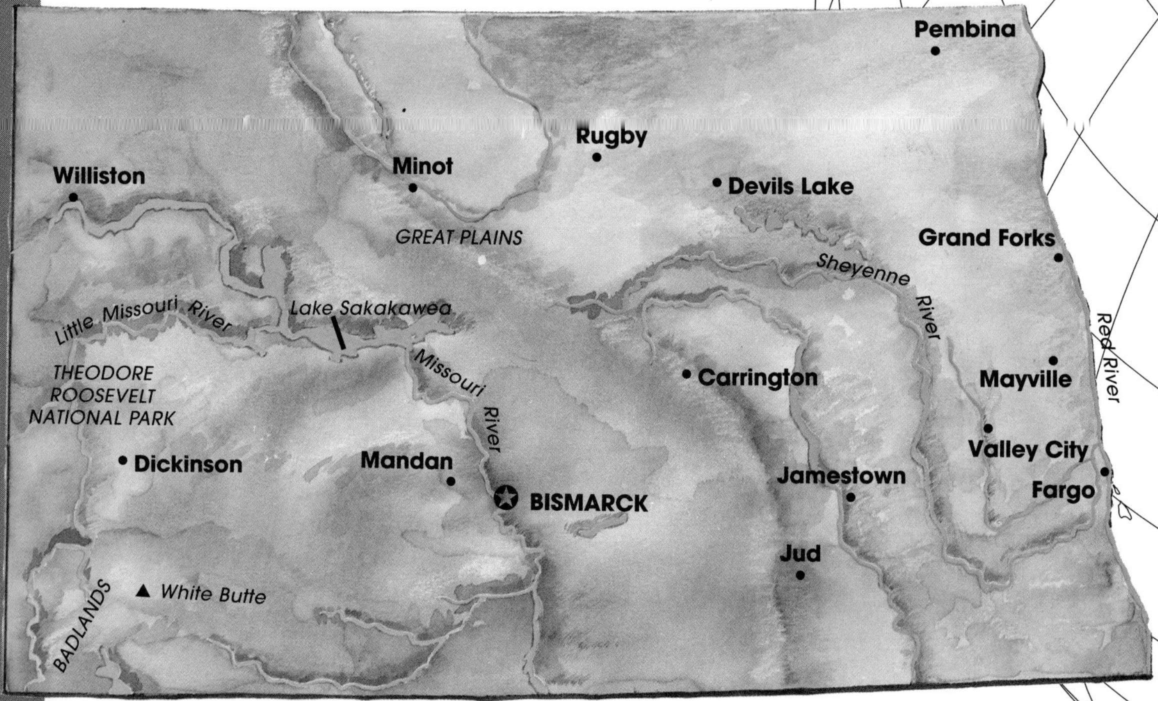

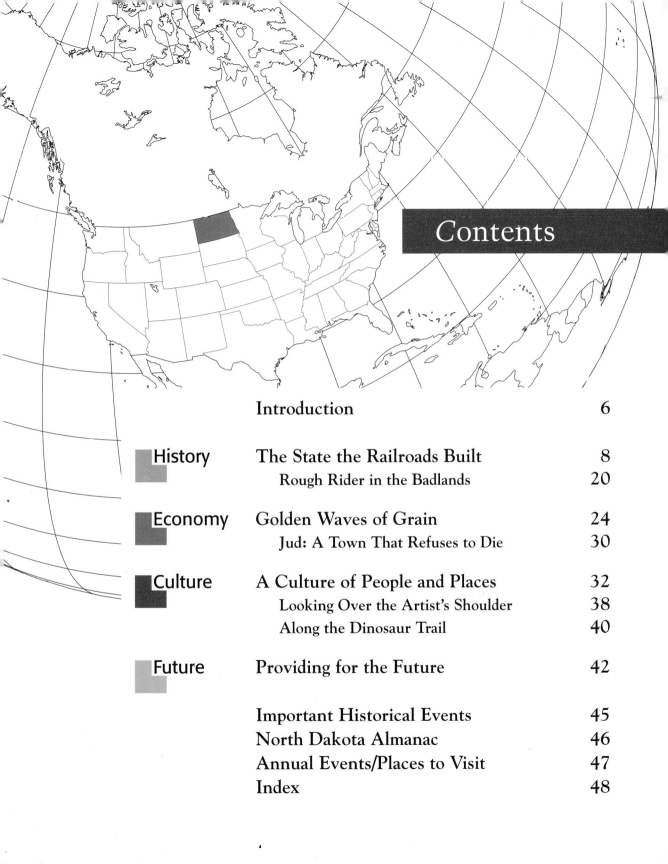

Contents

Introduction

Ice Age glaciers shaped North Dakota's land into hills, valleys, plains, streams, and rivers. The rich deposits that were left behind spurred the development of 33,000 farms and ranches stretching across nearly ninety percent of the state. In North Dakota the vitality of life waves from the fields of corn and wheat. Songbirds, eagles, and other birds fill the skies. More water birds hatch in North Dakota than in any other state. Deer and antelope grace the elm and aspen forests. Wildflowers and tall prairie grasses blanket the rolling landscape. The swift Missouri and Red rivers supply northern pike, perch, trout, and bass. Nature provides in North Dakota. It is a rich environment for all living things.

North Dakota farmers have long ago accepted the fact that the state's weather can often be severe.

North Dakota

Garrison Dam, Badlands, wheat

The State the Railroads Built

Native peoples inhabited present-day North Dakota long before European explorers arrived there. The Mandan, the Hidatsa, and the Arikara lived along the Knife and Missouri rivers in houses they made from mud and clay. These groups hunted, grew crops, and traded for furs, buffalo robes, and other goods. They also raised tobacco, corn, beans, and squash. Corn was especially important to the Arikara, and they honored corn in religious ceremonies. The Hidatsa found high-quality flint deposits along the Knife River and made flint tools and arrowheads.

Other groups of Native Americans moved into the North Dakota area after the Mandan, Hidatsa, and Arikara settled there. In the early 1600s, the Sioux spread west into the Dakotas from their homelands in what is present-day Minnesota. The Sioux were divided into subgroups such as the Dakota, Lakota, and Nakota. The name Dakota is a Sioux word meaning "allies" or "friends."

Theodore Roosevelt owned two ranches in this part of the Badlands during the 1880s. Today, this area is part of Theodore Roosevelt National Park.

Among William Clark's duties during the expedition were to keep a record of the trip and map the group's progress.

Meriwether Lewis was a soldier and explorer. Lewis gathered samples of plants, animals, and minerals as he and Clark traveled through the Louisiana Territory.

As the Sioux moved into the Devil's Lake area, they forced the Hidatsa to move where the Missouri and the Heart rivers meet. Eventually, the Sioux spread throughout the region and into the Great Plains.

In 1682 René Robert Cavelier, Sieur de La Salle, explored the Mississippi River from its northern source to the Gulf of Mexico. He claimed the entire Mississippi Valley for France, including all the rivers that drained into the Mississippi River. The area, called Louisiana, included part of what is now North Dakota. The French also claimed the northeastern area of present-day North Dakota as part of the territory. France later gave this territory to Great Britain in 1713.

The first European explorer to come to present-day North Dakota was Pierre Gaultier de Varennes, Sieur de la Vérendrye, in 1738. He, three of his sons, and a nephew traveled from Montreal, Canada, almost as far as today's Bismarck. They were looking for an overland route to the Pacific Ocean. Most of the party stayed for a time with the Mandan before returning to Canada. Two of the sons continued west.

In the 1790s traders and fur trappers followed La Vérendrye's route through Canada. They took furs they had received from the Native Americans in trade for goods.

In 1803 the United States bought Louisiana from France. One year later, President Thomas Jefferson sent out an expedition led by two men, Meriwether Lewis and William Clark, to explore the new land. Jefferson was interested in finding a water route to the

Pacific Ocean. Lewis and Clark reached present-day North Dakota in October 1804 by traveling along the Missouri River. Rather than continuing on through the winter, they built a fort on the bank of the Missouri River. They named it Fort Mandan, after the Native Americans who had befriended them. They left in April 1805. When they returned from the West the next year, they found the fort in ruins due to flooding and fire.

In 1812 a group of Scottish and Irish families from Canada established a permanent settlement at Pembina. This was the first European settlement in the North Dakota region. In 1818 the United States and Great Britain signed a treaty that set the international boundary between Canada and the United States at the 49th parallel. The new line set the present-day northern border of North Dakota.

Sakajewea, a Shoshone woman, and her husband Toussaint Charbonneau, a French trapper, met Lewis and Clark in the North Dakota region. She and her husband led the expedition to the West. Sakajewea's son was born on the journey.

In the early 1800s, businessmen such as John Jacob Astor became interested in the North Dakota region. Astor was the head of the American Fur Company, which competed with British companies for the fur trade in the West. In 1828 Astor's company built a trading post called Fort Union, where the Yellowstone River joins the Missouri River, near today's Williston. The fort became a thriving fur trading center.

Trade with the settlers brought guns, kettles, axes, and other goods to the Mandan, the Arikara, and the

Hidatsa. It also brought diseases such as smallpox. Native Americans had no resistance to these diseases, which were completely new to them. In 1837 smallpox almost completely wiped out the Mandan. Out of about 1,800 people, only a little over 100 survived. The Hidatsa and the Arikara suffered as well. The people who survived joined together at a community called Like-a-Fishhook Village, forming the Three Affiliated Tribes. The remaining members of the three groups moved to Fort Berthold, a reservation in northwest North Dakota.

During the 1850s, settlements and United States Army forts were being built alongside Devil's Lake and the Red and Missouri rivers. Steamboats brought more people and supplies. The Sioux, who had not become involved in the fur trade, saw what had happened to the other Native American groups. They saw the settlements as a danger to them.

In 1862 in Minnesota, fighting broke out between the Sioux and the settlers. Federal troops were called in to subdue the uprising. Many Sioux fled to join other

Pictured here from left to right are Hidatsa chief Crow Flies High, Arikara chief Sun-of-the-Star, and Hidatsa chief Crow Paunch and subchief Poor Wolf. These four men were leaders of the Three Affiliated Tribes during the late 1800s.

Sioux groups in present-day North Dakota. United States soldiers followed them, and a series of battles between soldiers and Sioux began. They continued off and on for nearly thirty more years.

Congress had formed the Dakota Territory in 1861. The Territory included present-day North Dakota and South Dakota and much of what are now Montana and Wyoming. In 1863 the Dakota Territory was opened for homesteading under the Homestead Act. It promised each homesteader 160 acres of free land if that homesteader lived on the land and improved it for five years. The offer of free land did not produce the desired result, however. The danger of attack by Native Americans was still very great. Also, transportation to the Territory was limited. There were few roads, and railroads had not yet reached that far west.

In the late 1860s, the United States government negotiated a treaty with some of the Sioux, giving them certain areas of land on which they could live. Settlers were supposed to stay out of those areas. The treaties only made for harder feelings between the federal government and Native Americans, however. Many settlers didn't obey the restrictions. In addition, the government constantly changed or rewrote the treaties, taking away more and more land and giving it to settlers.

In 1871 railroads reached the Minnesota side of the Red River. The federal government gave land grants to the Northern Pacific Railroad to lay tracks across the North Dakota Territory. The railroad built towns along the tracks and advertised in

The Whitestone Battlefield Historic Site marks one of the places the Sioux and the cavalry fought in the 1860s.

Settlers from Eastern Europe traveled together to North Dakota.

Europe to attract settlers to set up farms. Immigrants came from Germany, Norway, Poland, and Russia.

Huge wheat farms, called "bonanza farms," were established along the Red River Valley. The success of these bonanza farms drew even more settlers to the region. The Northern Pacific and the Great Northern railroads competed for contracts to haul the wheat from the region to markets in the east. Cattle ranchers bought grazing land for beef cattle. So many people moved to the Territory between 1878 and 1886 that this period was called the Dakota Boom.

By the late 1870s, people in the Dakota Territory realized how dependent they were on the railroads. The railroads had built their tracks from east to west in order to take crops to market. There were few north-south routes. Because the settlers in the north had little contact with those in the south, they asked Congress to divide the territory into two parts. In November 1889, by alphabetical order, North Dakota became the thirty-ninth state and South Dakota became the fortieth.

North Dakota grew quickly. By 1910 its population reached over five hundred thousand. Most of these people were farmers. Based on the way North Dakota's economy had developed, many businesses outside the state—mainly in Minnesota—controlled services that North Dakota farmers needed. North Dakotans grew the wheat, but Minnesota railroads carried the grain to market, and Minnesota businesses stored it or turned it into flour. North Dakotans borrowed money to develop their land or to plant their crops, but Minnesota banks loaned the money. Cattle ranchers had similar problems. Minnesota businesses had too much control over the way things were done in North Dakota.

In 1915 thousands of North Dakota farmers joined together to form the Nonpartisan League (NPL). The league supported the idea of state-owned banks, grain elevators, flour mills, packing houses, and storage plants. The league also supported political candidates. In 1916 the winning candidate for governor had strong NPL support. In 1919 the North Dakota legislature acted on the NPL's

The Nonpartisan League was a grass-roots movement of people working together to better their lives.

ideas. The legislature also created a program to help disabled farmers, a hail insurance program, and a state-supported home-building association. The NPL lost political power within a few years, but many of its goals remained. In 1927 the North Dakota Farmers Union was founded to carry on the NPL traditions.

In 1930 the entire country was hit by the Great Depression. Banks and industries across the country closed, and millions of people were unemployed. By 1932, many of the banks in North Dakota had gone bankrupt, wiping out the savings of thousands of families. The federal government, led by President Franklin D. Roosevelt, began programs to help people by providing them with government jobs. In the 1930s, many people in North Dakota were involved in some kind of government program.

A seven-year drought fell over the Great Plains. As the drought continued, more plants died. Their roots couldn't hold the soil in place. Winds blew away the topsoil. Farming was impossible. For many people, government programs were not an answer. Between 1930 and 1940, nearly forty thousand people left North Dakota for someplace to start over.

Those farmers who stayed through the hard times began developing a method called "dry farming." This farming method helped them get the most possible use of North Dakota's low levels of rainfall. The state also developed irrigation projects and programs to prevent soil erosion. A state commission to conserve water was set up in 1937.

In 1941 the United States entered World War II, and North Dakota's vast wheat fields helped feed troops. In 1946, one year after the war ended, the federal government began construction on the Garrison Dam near Riverdale. The dam provided flood control, hydroelectric power, and farm irrigation. Agriculture continued to grow after the war, but farmers were using more machines. That meant that they needed fewer workers. Unemployment rose. Small farms closed down or were bought by larger farms. People began to move to urban areas, such as Fargo and Bismarck, to find work.

In 1951 oil was discovered south of Tioga in western North Dakota. This oil field extended across the

The Garrison Dam took fourteen years to complete.

17

western half of North Dakota and into Canada, Montana, and South Dakota. The Williston Field, as it is called, made North Dakota one of the largest producers of crude petroleum in the nation.

North Dakota began an economic development program in 1957 to attract new industries to the state. The program was very successful, and for more than ten years North Dakota had the highest growth rate of all the states.

In the 1960s, the federal government contributed to the state's growth by building Air Force bases near Grand Forks and Minot. In addition, the government constructed several intercontinental ballistic missile sites throughout the state. To help North Dakota's farmers, the state began the Garrison Diversion Project in 1968. Its system of irrigation canals was designed to bring water from the Missouri River to farms in the state's central region. However, opposition to the program resulted in a limitation of its goals.

The 1970s were good for North Dakotans. The Williston oil field was so productive that by 1971 about 14 counties had oil wells. The cost of oil became very high in the early 1970s. The high cost spurred a national interest in developing other sources of energy such as natural gas and coal. North Dakota has large deposits of natural gas and a type of coal called lignite. Scientists believed that lignite could be converted to a gas to be used for energy. With funding from the federal government, research began to find the best way to "gasify" lignite coal.

By the mid-1980s the price of oil and gas fell, and the economy of the state suffered. Requests for federal support for the lignite research project were denied.

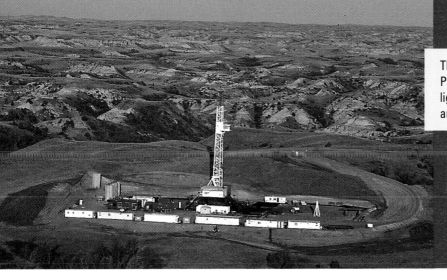

The Great Plains Synfuels Plant in Beulah converts lignite coal to natural gas and other products.

However, the project was purchased by the Dakota Gassification Company in 1988, and research continued. A gassification plant was built, and today coal gassification and its many by-products have been very successful.

North Dakota also has coal-burning electric generation plants. They supply electricity to North Dakota, Minnesota, and several surrounding states.

Another drought hit the state in 1988, and about forty percent of the spring wheat crop was destroyed. Conservation and irrigation systems couldn't solve the problem. Then, in 1993 heavy rains caused severe floods along the Missouri and Red rivers. The federal government declared parts of North Dakota disaster areas.

Nevertheless, North Dakotans retain a positive outlook for the years ahead. Agriculture is still a part of the hearts and minds of North Dakotans, many of whom are descendants of settlers to this region. Clean air, open spaces, and a tradition of people working together are qualities of North Dakota that are just as strong now as they ever were.

19

Rough Rider in the Badlands

By the time Theodore Roosevelt was 27 years old, he had already traveled to a number of foreign countries, graduated from Harvard University, and written a book. He had also served in the New York state legislature for three years. Roosevelt had a bright future, and it seemed like nothing could stand in his way. Then, on February 14, 1884, tragedy struck. Both his mother and his wife died on the same night. Theodore Roosevelt was crushed by the loss. His grief was so great he could not think about continuing as he had been. He turned his back on his former life by retiring from politics. He wanted to get away to a place where he could put his life back in order. His search for the right place brought him to the North Dakota

Roosevelt was a real working cowboy when he lived in North Dakota.

When Roosevelt first came to North Dakota, he stayed in the Maltese Cross Cabin.

Badlands, in the area along the Little Missouri River.

The Badlands area is scored by deep gullies and sharp outcroppings of red scoria clay. In the late 1880s, this dramatic wilderness was teeming with buffalo and other wildlife. It was the idea of hunting buffalo that brought Roosevelt to the Badlands. Once there, however, he became fascinated by the beauty of its landscape. Roosevelt decided to stay.

Theodore Roosevelt wasn't one for doing things only partway. He started two cattle ranches and became deeply involved in performing the day-to-day chores. Roosevelt spent 14-to-16 hour days on horseback, helping the other cowboys tend to his cattle. For a short time he was also a deputy sheriff, and he helped law officers capture a band of outlaws! Roosevelt also continued to write. Within the first six months of his arrival in North Dakota, Theodore Roosevelt wrote a biography of Senator Thomas Hart Benton. He later wrote a book called *The Winning of the West*.

The worst winter in frontier history fell upon the Badlands in 1886.

Roosevelt thought that the Badlands was one of the most amazing places he had ever seen.

It became known as the "Blue Winter." At times the temperature fell to 45 degrees below zero. The people of the town of Medora, near Roosevelt's ranch, had to board up their windows to keep out starving cattle. In the face of that harsh winter, ranchers had to sit by while their herds froze to death. Along with the other ranchers in the area, Roosevelt had to admit defeat.

But, in another sense, it wasn't a defeat at all. Roosevelt returned to New York in 1886. He married again and returned to public life. He was appointed Civil Service Commissioner in 1888. He held that occupation until he became president of the New York City Board of Police Commissioners in 1893. Three years later he became Assistant Secretary of the Navy. When the United States declared war on Spain in 1898, Roosevelt resigned so that he could join the fight. Part of the Spanish-American War was fought in

Cuba, a Spanish colony. Roosevelt formed the First Volunteer Cavalry Regiment from volunteers, some of whom were former college athletes and cowboys from the West. They became known as the "Rough Riders." On July 1, 1898, the Rough Riders became nationally famous when they overtook a Spanish stronghold on San Juan Hill.

In 1900 Theodore Roosevelt was elected Vice President of the United States under President William McKinley. Only six months after being elected President, McKinley was assassinated, and Roosevelt became the twenty-sixth President of the United States. In 1904 he was elected to serve another term. Roosevelt credited his success in part to his years in the Badlands. He said that what he learned during those years in North Dakota prepared him for becoming President of the United States.

As usual, Theodore Roosevelt followed up his feelings with action. In 1905 Roosevelt established the United States Forest Service and opened five new national parks across the country. He declared millions of acres of land as national forests and 11 sites as national monuments. He used his authority as President to create the first federal bird reserves and established the first national game preserves.

The Badlands that brought Theodore Roosevelt so much pleasure have not changed that much. The drama, the mystery, and the stark beauty are still there. Winding through the Badlands of North Dakota is a protected area designated as the Theodore Roosevelt National Park.

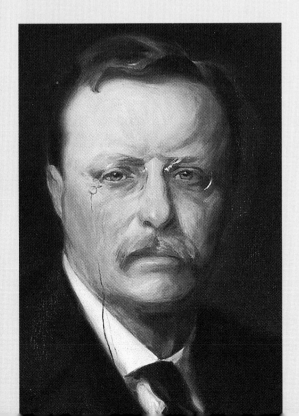

Theodore Roosevelt believed that what he had learned during his years in North Dakota prepared him for the presidency.

Golden Waves of Grain

Many former agricultural states have shifted away from farming and ranching to manufacturing. But that hasn't happened in North Dakota. There is manufacturing in the state, but agriculture is still the most important part of the economy. One reason manufacturing has not become a larger part of the state's economy is its limited transportation systems.

Transportation makes it possible to bring raw materials into an area and move finished products out of it. North Dakota never developed a transportation network that would serve markets within the state or in neighboring states. Today, North Dakota's two major east-west highways run close to the east-west railroad tracks, and transportation in the state is still limited. In addition, North Dakota is far away from most of the major cities in the United States. Limited transportation and great distances to large consumer markets have kept North Dakota from diversifying or varying its economic choices.

The south-central area of North Dakota provides good pastures for raising dairy cattle.

Sunflowers produce seeds that can be eaten or can be turned into oil for cooking and for dressings.

Agriculture accounts for about eight percent of North Dakota's Gross State Product (GSP). Gross State Product is the dollar value of all the goods and services produced in a year in a state.

There are about 33,000 farms and ranches in North Dakota. Wheat is the most important crop raised in the state. North Dakota farmers raise spring wheat, drumwheat, and many other varieties of the crop. Durum wheat is used to make pasta products such as noodles and spaghetti. North Dakota is second only to Kansas in the amount of wheat grown in the United States.

North Dakota is the country's number one producer of barley and sunflower seeds. Honey and flaxseed are also leading crops. Flaxseed is the source of linseed oil, and linseed oil is one of the important elements in the manufacture of paint. North Dakota is also a major producer of oats, rye, beans, corn, potatoes, and sugar beets.

Wheat is grown on the Great Plains in North Dakota.

When coal is strip-mined, the land is dug away layer by layer. As coal is revealed, it is hauled away. The state now strictly regulates this type of mining because it can cause so much damage to the environment.

It also produces hay, which is used to feed beef cattle. North Dakota's ranches produce mainly beef cattle. However, there are also a large number of dairy farms. Milk is the state's second most important livestock product.

Mining is also a major part of North Dakota's economy. It accounts for about 12 percent of the Gross State Product. When oil was discovered in the Williston Basin in the 1950s, North Dakota became one of the most important oil-producing states in the country. Today, oil is North Dakota's most important mineral product. Most oil is mined in the western part of the state. North Dakota also has about two thirds of all the lignite coal deposits presently found in the country. North Dakota uses much of its lignite coal to run its

Food processing is an important part of North Dakota manufacturing. These pasta noodles are made from durum wheat grown in the state.

power plants. The state produces so much electricity that it sells half of its production to other states in the Midwest. In the southwestern part of the state there are natural gas deposits.

Only about eight percent of the state's GSP comes from manufacturing. Many of North Dakota's industries are related to agriculture and mining. North Dakota processes its sugar beets to make sugar and its grains to make pasta and other products. North Dakota livestock provide the state with dairy and meat products. In Mandan, oil refineries produce petroleum. Other North Dakota companies manufacture printed materials and transportation equipment, such as buses and aircraft parts.

Service industries make up the largest portion of the state's GSP—about 72 percent. In service industries people don't make products. Instead, they provide services such as working in a department store, a bank, or a repair shop.

Wholesale and retail trade is the most important category of North Dakota's service industries. Wholesale trade involves selling large quantities of products to stores. Retail trade is the business of selling these goods to individual customers. North Dakota wholesalers provide petroleum products to companies or businesses that sell them to customers at service stations.

The second most important category of North Dakota's service economy includes finance, insurance, and real estate. People in this category lend money to farmers, who then buy seed for the coming year or purchase farm machinery. These businesses also insure property and equipment and buy and sell land.

The third largest category of service industries is community, social, and personal services. Included in this category are hospitals, clinics, and dentist offices. The main medical centers in North Dakota are in Fargo and Bismarck. Government services make up the fourth largest category of North Dakota's service industries. People in this category may work for the local, state, or federal government. Local and state workers include police officers, firefighters, and teachers. In North Dakota, federal government employees work at the four Native American reservations as well as at the wildlife refuges and the national parks.

A large part of the state's tourism income is calculated as part of its service industries. That's because tourists use so many service businesses. They stay at motels, buy hunting equipment, and pay fees at national parks or boat-rental agencies. North Dakota estimates that tourism contributes more than $900 million to the state's economy.

North Dakota's economy has been fairly steady for several years now. The state has a strong economic development department that is working to draw more industries to the state. Today, North Dakota depends heavily on agriculture. However, if the demand for products falls, or if there is a bad growing season, the whole state suffers. An economy with a wider variety of businesses will protect North Dakota citizens from hard times.

Camping is a popular recreation for tourists who want to enjoy North Dakota's great outdoors.

Jud: A Town That Refuses to Die

Jud is a tiny town in southeastern North Dakota. It has a population of about 100 people. For a long time the town has struggled to survive against what seems like overwhelming odds. In many ways its story is the story of many small towns all over America.

For years Jud was a resource for neighboring farms—a place to pick up groceries and supplies. Two hundred farmers in the area stored their grain at the grain elevator in town. The Burlington-Northern Railroad regularly stopped at Jud, loaded the grain, and carried it to market. However, over the years rail service diminished. The railroad company said that coming all the way out to small towns like Jud cost too much money. Finally Burlington-Northern abandoned the line and farmers had to take their grain to train depots farther away. Some communities along the line did not survive. But the community spirit in the people of Jud was too strong. The town did not give up.

In the center of the town is the Jud Cafe. Farmers used to come in to drink coffee and visit with their neighbors. People used the cafe to find out

Over the years, the Jud Cafe has changed names and changed owners, but its importance to the community has never changed.

what was happening in their community. Who got married? Who needed a hand at harvest? Whose daughter or son graduated from the University of North Dakota? Whatever the people needed or wanted to know about each other, they found out at the cafe.

When the railroad stopped serving the town, fewer and fewer people came into the cafe, and the owners finally said they were going to close it down. So, a group of women in the town took it over for a while, rather than let it die. Now the Jud Cafe is owned by the community.

Lately Jud has welcomed the addition of the Great Plains Assistance Dogs Foundation. This is a school that trains dogs to help people who are disabled. It is similar to schools that provide seeing-eye dogs for people who are blind. People who use these dogs may be deaf or have some other physical disability. Some people in Jud volunteer to take part in the early training of the dogs. The dog lives with the volunteer, learning good social skills and obedience that comes from careful and loving discipline.

The people of Jud are determined to stay together. They want to keep their community and their way of life. That way of life depends on the survival of places such as the Jud Cafe and other long-established places in town. One resident put it plainly: "Jud is the type of community that . . . the people really work together to keep it going. And that's what you need, you know."

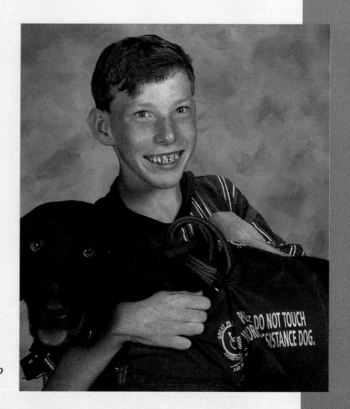

Great Plains Assistance Foundation Dogs are trained to retrieve objects, open doors, and alert their owners to sounds. They also provide excellent companionship.

A Culture of People and Places

When some people refer to the culture of a place, they mean the things that make it different from other places. What makes each place different is the land and the people who carved out their lives from the land.

Native Americans were the first to make their cultural imprint on North Dakota. They had a close relationship with nature. They respected the animals they hunted and thanked them for providing meat for food and skins for clothing. They believed that all creatures had an equal share in nature and that all things, even the wind and the rain, had a purpose.

Today there are four Native American reservations in North Dakota, and all of them hold special events throughout the year. Everyone is welcome to attend their traditional celebrations, called powwows. During powwows, Native Americans dance, sing, and join in traditional storytelling. A variety of traditional clothing worn during powwow celebrations adds to the excitement. For example, the grass dancer wears a colorful fringe that resembles grass blowing in the

Sioux, Ojibwa, Arikara, Hidatsa, and Mandan have maintained many of their cultural traditions, such as dancing. Traditional dancers tell a story, using precise, rhythmic footwork.

Sitting Bull was one leader of the Sioux forces that defeated Lieutenant Colonel George Armstrong Custer at the Battle of the Little Bighorn, in Montana. At the time, Custer and his troops were stationed at Fort Abraham Lincoln in North Dakota.

wind. Another dancer wears a circular bustle of eagle feathers when telling the story of a battle or a hunt through a dance.

Another group that made their presence known on the land was the United States Cavalry. North Dakota was the site of many confrontations between Native Americans and the cavalry. The most famous cavalry member was Lieutenant Colonel George Armstrong Custer. Custer was sent out to North Dakota after the Civil War to lead troops in the war with the Sioux. His headquarters was at Fort Abraham Lincoln, not far from Bismarck.

Fort Abraham Lincoln is the partially restored home of Custer's 7th U.S. Cavalry. Visitors to this fort can see reenactments of daily life at a typical fort of the 1800s. Uniformed soldiers parade their horses, set up a tent camp in the square, and perform activities that Custer and his men would have done. The restoration also includes the home that Custer and his wife lived in, the commissary, and the soldier's barracks. Fort Lincoln has been honored as one of the stops on the American Legacy Tour, a series of sites throughout the state that let visitors get a real-life view of how North Dakota was settled.

Buffalo are found in the parks and wildlife refuges in the state, and on the Fort Berthold Reservation of the Three Affiliated Tribes.

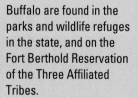

Immigrants from European countries began arriving in North Dakota in the late nineteenth century. One of the largest groups of immigrants in the state came from Norway. At one time there were over fifty Norwegian newspapers in North Dakota. Norwegian is still the second language in some small North Dakota communities. It was also taught in North Dakota schools, and the University of North Dakota now offers classes in Norwegian language and literature. In June the Scandinavian Hjemkomst Festival is held in Fargo. Traditional dances, music, and food are enjoyed in a celebration of the Scandinavian heritage of many North Dakotans.

This photo shows a replica of a Native American home at the Knife Indian Village National Historic Site near Stanton.

Other immigrants came to North Dakota from Germany and Russia. The Russians settled in the south-central area of the state. At the time, Ukraine was part of Russia and at the Ukrainian Cultural Institute in Dickinson there are concerts, dances, displays, and special classes on Ukrainian art. Similar festivals celebrate German heritage and that of the French fur traders. At Fort Union, the annual Trading Post Rendezvous re-creates the life of the fur-trading days.

North Dakota's culture is also celebrated through restorations such as the Billings Country Courthouse Museum in Medora. The museum features displays about the life of early ranchers. Medora itself is a

This rodeo cowboy is performing in the steer wrestling event. In steer wrestling, the cowboy must grab the steer's horns and wrestle it to the ground.

restored cowboy boomtown. At Bonanzaville USA in West Fargo there is a restoration of a typical pioneer village. It includes artifacts from the days of North Dakota's bonanza farms.

North Dakota's protected landmarks are also a part of the state's culture. By protecting these areas, North Dakotans preserve their historic wilderness as well as ensure that future change to the area will only develop naturally. Perhaps the most famous land area in North Dakota is the Badlands. Native Americans believed this area was sacred ground. North Dakotans have protected this area as part of Theodore Roosevelt National Park. The Badlands is a long narrow valley about 190 miles long and from 6 to 20 miles wide. The land is made up of sand, shale, and clay. Erosion from wind and water have carved this land into hills, domes, and buttes. Some of these land formations reveal bands of various types of earth that have settled on top of each other. There are deposits of lignite coal in the Badlands, and some of these deposits have been burning underground for many years. The gasses from the burning coal have colored the soil above it pink or bright red.

Another land area unique to North Dakota is the Missouri Couteau area. On the western side of this region is the Missouri River, and on the eastern side is the Sheyenne River. Every spring and fall the land and rivers form the busiest highway in the United States for millions of migrating birds! More waterfowl, such as ducks and geese, hatch in North Dakota than anywhere else in the United States. Hunters are allowed in certain areas, but others are reserved as wildlife refuges. In these places, the only shooting that's allowed is with a camera.

The people of North Dakota point with pride at the various elements that make up their culture. They can view or take part in a rodeo, participate in a powwow, or spend a weekend fishing, skiing, or exploring. Where culture is concerned, it is the parts that make up the whole in North Dakota.

North Dakota is a haven for ducks and geese because of its many wetlands. These snow geese are flying over J. Clark Salyer National Wildlife Refuge.

Looking Over the Artist's Shoulder

It is common knowledge that different people can look at a place and see different things. Sometimes what they see is what interests them most about the place. If the person who is looking is an artist, what will he or she see? Jackie McElroy is a silkscreen artist. Silkscreening is a printmaking technique in which paint or ink is pressed through a piece of silk onto a surface. Her first reaction to eastern North Dakota wasn't very positive. When she looked out over the prairies and fields, she saw empty and colorless land. After living in the area for about four years, however, Jackie began to change her mind. She saw colors that she hadn't been aware of before. "I started to pay attention to the way the light changed things, and I really finally decided that North Dakota, this end of North Dakota, was surprisingly beautiful. The color of it."

As an artist who expresses herself with shades of color, small variations in color became important to Jackie. "In the fall particularly, there are . . . over a hundred shades of brown and violet that you'll see across the pastures and in some of the stubblefields. Then there are yellows that I've seen only in some late nineteenth, early twentieth century French paintings. There are greens and shades of greens that exist nowhere else. . . . You can see them because the sunlight is . . . so clear, unpolluted, brilliant, and in this northern latitude [the sunlight] hangs at a different angle, I think, than on either coast."

The next thing that impressed Jackie was the geometric shapes built right into the land. The fields were

Jackie McElroy learned to appreciate the subtle beauty of North Dakota.

38

This 1991 painting by Jackie McElroy is called North Dakota Tree Project #1.

set out in perfect rectangles and were neatly aligned, one after the other. Those straight lines stretched on and on for as far as she could see, creating a vast, flat, geometric plain. The things Jackie was seeing were affecting her art. "I got kind of enchanted . . . by the flat."

Jackie knows there's a reason for those amazing straight lines. They were created when the territorial government laid out homesteads in the late 1800s. The government measured mile-square sections along straight lines. All the roads, with very few exceptions, are perfectly straight and run north, south, east, and west. The only thing that varied the straight lines was an occasional creek.

Now, Jackie uses what she sees in her silkscreens. She borrows North Dakota's delicate colors and long straight lines and works them into her art. For Jackie McElroy, all it took was a second look.

Jackie McElroy silkscreened this harvest scene in 1981. Harvest time is one of North Dakota's most colorful seasons.

Along the Dinosaur Trail

Cowboys still work on the large farms and ranches of southwestern North Dakota. Not much about the cowboy's job has changed in more than a hundred years. But a few North Dakota cowboys have found a brand-new reason to "ride the range." Cowboys and other volunteers have been trained by scientists at North Dakota's Pioneer Trails Regional Museum to be dinosaur hunters. Dinosaur fossils are a fairly common sight in North Dakota, but you have to know where to look.

Sixty-eight million years ago, the area that is now southwestern North Dakota was located at the edge of a shallow sea that covered most of the central part of North America. Many streams and rivers also flowed through the area. A wide variety of plants sprang up on the swampy land. Then animals—including dinosaurs—began arriving in search of food. The muddy soil preserved the remains of these animals. Over time, the mud dried up and was buried under layers of rock and dirt.

Dinosaur fossils have been found at more than a thousand sites all over the world. Not many of these places are more important to paleontologists, the scientists who study fossils, than North Dakota. For one thing, an impressive variety of fossil remains has been found in the state. In addition to more than a dozen different kinds of dinosaurs, paleontologists have found crocodiles, lizards, fish, and plants that lived around the same time. Ancient rhinoceroses, camels, cats, and horses have also been found.

Another thing that sets North Dakota apart from many other fossil-producing areas is the number of complete skeletons that have been found in the state. At the Dakota Dinosaur Museum in Dickinson, the

In 1964 parts of a triceratops skull was found at this Pioneer Trails dig site. The triceratops lived millions of years ago when North Dakota had warm weather, swamps, and abundant vegetation.

This mastodon skeleton is on display at the North Dakota Heritage Center. Mastodons, which were very much like present-day elephants, became extinct about ten thousand years ago.

Paleontologists carefully look for fossils at a Pioneer Trails dig site.

complete skeletons of 10 dinosaurs, a rhino, and a bison are on display. Some of the skeletons are real, and some are replicas or sculptures. If the *Tyrannosaurus rex* skeleton found near Rhame, North Dakota, is complete, it will be only the third whole "T. rex" ever found.

All of the dinosaurs found in North Dakota have something in common: They were among the last dinosaurs to roam the earth. About 65 million years ago, something happened to cause the extinction of dinosaurs and many other living things. Scientists have been trying to solve this mystery for years. North Dakota may hold the key. And the person who finds it just might be a cowboy.

Providing for the Future

North Dakota has many resources—it has rich soil, a wealth of minerals, and a clean environment. But North Dakota's biggest resource may be its young people. Almost 90 percent of high school students in North Dakota stay in school and graduate. What's more, many high school graduates continue their education by attending the state's colleges and technical schools. But all too often, once these young people are finished with their education, they don't stay in North Dakota. They move to other states, where there are more job opportunities.

North Dakotans know their state can't afford to lose the great potential of these young minds. The state is working very hard to diversify its economy. To do this, North Dakota is "advertising" its benefits to various businesses outside the state. And it has a lot to offer. Today's businesses need a great deal of energy, and North Dakota's dams and power plants provide more than enough electricity for added businesses. Perhaps more importantly, North Dakota also offers

There are no indications that the future will change North Dakotans' love for the wide-open spaces and natural environment.

These students at the University of North Dakota are preparing themselves for a bright future. State officials hope students' plans include careers in North Dakota.

energy in the form of well-trained, hard-working employees.

Many businesses today use computers and sophisticated information systems to send out information, ideas, designs, or data. This way of doing business is part of what has been called the "information superhighway." All some businesses need is office space, telephone lines, and as many personal computers as employees. Many of these businesses are an extension of the service industries that already play a large part in North Dakota's economy. Businesses like these are ideally suited to North Dakota. One major reason is that they do not intrude on farmland or pollute the environment.

Some North Dakotans say that life in their state has always been challenging. They have faced blizzards, floods, and drought. Now North Dakota may be facing its greatest challenge: keeping its young people working at home.

1682 René-Robert Cavelier, Sieur de La Salle, claims the Mississippi Valley for France, including most of present-day North Dakota.

1738 French-Canadian Pierre Gaultier de Varennes, Sieur de la Vérendrye, is the first to explore the North Dakota region.

1742 La Vérendrye's sons return to the North Dakota region.

1763 The Treaty of Paris gives the northern section of the North Dakota region to Great Britain.

1797 David Thompson, of the North West Company, maps present-day North Dakota. Charles Chaboillez establishes a trading post at Pembina.

1804 Meriwether Lewis and William Clark pass through present-day North Dakota.

1812 Scottish and Irish settlers establish the area's first permanent European settlement in Pembina.

1818 A treaty with Great Britain gives the United States the northeastern section of present-day North Dakota.

1819 The American Fur Company builds Fort Union on the Yellowstone River.

1831 The American Fur Company builds Fort Clark on the Missouri River.

1832 The *Yellowstone*, the first steamboat up the Missouri River in North Dakota, reaches Fort Union.

1851 The First Fort Laramie Treaty defines the Three Affiliated Tribes' Territory.

1861 Congress creates the Dakota Territory.

1863 The Dakota Territory is opened to homesteaders.

1868 Joseph Rolette locates the first homestead in the northwestern Red River Valley. Sioux reservations are established by the Second Fort Laramie Treaty.

1873 The Northern Pacific Railway reaches Bismarck.

1889 Congress divides the territory into North Dakota and South Dakota. North Dakota enters the Union as the thirty-ninth state. The capital is Bismarck.

1915 The Nonpartisan League is founded.

1919 The Bank of North Dakota, a state-owned bank, is started in Bismarck.

1922 The state-owned North Dakota State Mill and Elevator is opened in Grand Forks.

1929 A seven-year drought begins.

1946 Construction of the Garrison Dam begins.

1951 Oil is discovered near Tioga.

1953 The first electric power is generated by Garrison Dam.

1957 An economic development commission is established to attract businesses to the state.

1962 A crude-oil pipeline is completed from Lignite to Clearbrook, Minnesota.

1968 The state authorizes the Garrison Diversion Project to irrigate 250,000 acres of farmland.

1988 A severe drought damages millions of acres in the state.

1993 Heavy rains cause floods along the Missouri River. Many North Dakota counties are declared federal disaster areas.

The state flag is a modified version of the seal of the United States on a field of blue. Below the seal is a banner with the words "North Dakota."

North Dakota Almanac

Nickname. The Flickertail State

Capital. Bismarck

State Bird. Western meadowlark

State Flower. Wild prairie rose

State Tree. American elm

State Motto. Liberty and Union, Now and Forever, One and Inseparable

State Song. "North Dakota Hymn"

State Abbreviations. N. Dak. or N.D. (traditional); ND (postal)

Statehood. November 2, 1889, the 39th state

Government. Congress: U.S. senators, 2; U.S. representatives, 1. State Legislature: senators, 49; representatives, 98. Counties: 53

Area. 70,704 sq mi (183,123 sq km), 17th in size among the states

Greatest Distances. north/south, 212 mi (341 km); east/west, 360 mi (580 km)

Elevation. Highest: White Butte, 3,506 ft (1,069 m). Lowest: 750 ft (229 m)

Population. 641,364 (2% decrease over 1980), 47th among the states. Density: 9 persons per sq mi (4 persons per sq km). Distribution: 47% rural, 53% urban. 1980 Census: 652,695

Economy. *Agriculture*: wheat, beef cattle, sunflower seeds, barley, hay, milk, sugar beets, potatoes, flaxseed. *Manufacturing*: food products, nonelectric machinery, printed materials, stone, clay and glass products. *Mining*: petroleum, coal, natural gas liquids, sand and gravel

State Seal

State Bird:
Western meadowlark

State Flower:
Wild prairie rose

Annual Events

★ North Dakota Winter Show in Valley City (March)

★ Time Out and Wacipi, Native American Days in Grand Forks (April)

★ Fort Seward Wagon Train in Jamestown (June)

★ Fort Union Rendezvous (June)

★ International Peace Garden Music Camp (June)

★ Roughrider Days in Dickinson (July)

★ Sodbuster Days in Fort Ransom State Park (July)

★ Folkfest in Bismarck (August)

★ United Tribes International Powwow in Bismarck (September)

★ Makoti Threshing Bee in Makoti (October)

Places to Visit

★ Billings Country Courthouse Museum, in Medora

★ Bonanzaville USA, in West Fargo

★ Chateau De Mores, near Medora

★ Dakota Dinosaur Museum in Dickinson

★ Fort Abraham Lincoln, near Mandan

★ International Peace Garden, north of Bottineau

★ National Buffalo Museum and Pioneer Village in Jamestown

★ Theodore Roosevelt National Park in the Badlands

★ Ukrainian Cultural Institute in Dickinson

★ Writing Rock, near Grenora

Index